THE BUILDER

THROUGH HISTORY

Richard Wood

with illustrations by Mark Peppé

Wayland

JOURNEY THROUGH HISTORY
The Builder Through History
The Farmer Through History
The Inventor Through History
The Sailor Through History
The Soldier Through History

Series editor: William Wharfe
Editor: Kathryn Smith and
            Catherine Baxter
Designer: Robert Wheeler

Typeset in the UK by Dorchester
Typesetting Group Ltd
Printed in Italy by G. Canale &
C.S.p.A., Turin

First published in 1994 by
Wayland (Publishers) Limited
61 Western Road, Hove
East Sussex BN3 1JD, England

© Copyright 1994 Wayland
(Publishers) Limited

**British Library Cataloguing in
Publication Data**
  Wood, Richard
  Builder Through History. –
  (Journey Through History series)
  I. Title II. Smith, Tony III. Series
  690

ISBN 0 7502 0971 2

Picture acknowledgements
The Bodleian Library 28; Cephas 5,
10, 41; Bruce Coleman 16, 28, 34;
Dixon 19, 34; Eye Ubiquitous 32;
Mary Evans 36 (top); Sonia Halliday
25; Holford 10, 12, 16 (top), 17, 22,
25; Ronald Sheridan 8, 9 (top), 33,
36 (bottom); Tony Stone Worldwide
4, 6, 32 (both), 37, 38, 40; Wayland
Picture Library 9 (bottom), 13, 21,
24, 29, 42, 45.

Text acknowledgements
The publishers have attempted to
contact all copyright holders of the
quotations in this book, and apolo-
gize if there have been any over-
sights.
The publishers gratefully acknowl-
edge permission from the following
to reproduce copyright material:
Phaidon Press, for an extract quoted
in *The Story of Architecture,* by
Patrick Nuttgens, 1983; Penguin, for
extracts from: 1) Herodotus
Histories, translated by Aubrey de
Selincourt, 1954, 2) Plutarch,
Pericles, from *The Rise and Fall of
Athens,* translated by Ian Scott-
Kilvert, 1960, 3) Tacitus *On Britain
and Germany,* translated by H
Mattingly, 1948; Hulton for extracts
from Statius *Silvae,* IV, iii, quoted in
These were the Romans, by GIF
Tingay & J Badcock, 1972; British
Museum Press, for extracts from
Gervase, *Chronicles,* quoted in
Masons and Sculptors by Nicola
Coldstream, 1991; Hamish
Hamilton, for Nahuatl poem, quoted
in *Cortez and the Downfall of the
Aztec Empire,* p.99, by John
Manchip White, 1971; Bromley
Library Service, for an extract quot-
ed in *Palace of the People,* by
Graham Reeves, 1986.

Contents

Introduction

Ever since people began to farm land and settle in one place, they have needed to build shelters to live in. At first, most people built their own homes, using whatever materials they could find close at hand. Mud, wood, straw and reeds are readily available throughout most of the world. These materials were easy to use, did not cost much, and could be quite strong and waterproof. In some places, builders still use traditional methods and materials like these.

As communities became larger and more organized, bigger buildings were needed. These were not the responsibility of any one family. They were used by chiefs or kings, or by the whole community on special occasions and for religious gatherings.

Prehistoric stone circles, like Castlerigg in England, may have been used for religious gatherings.

Some people began to learn the special skills needed to build these larger buildings, and were paid for their work. The age of the professional builder had arrived.

Some buildings, like tombs, temples and churches, were so important that they needed to be very strong and beautiful. Such buildings were usually built in stone. This kind of building work required people with many different skills, to quarry, cut and carve the stone.

Over the past two centuries, builders have begun to make more use of materials like iron, steel, concrete and glass. These materials require new knowledge on the part of designers, engineers and building workers.

Most buildings have many different builders. There is the person who orders the building or pays for it, as the Egyptian Pharaoh Cheops built the Great Pyramid. Then there is the architect who draws the designs for the building, and calculates

Churches, like Segovia Cathedral in Spain, completed many years ago, still dominate the surrounding buildings.

the measurements and quantities of materials needed, like Gustav Eiffel who built the Eiffel Tower in Paris. Finally, there are all the craftsmen and workers who do the physical hard work of constructing the building on the site. You will discover more about all three kinds of builder in this book. Which type of builder would you prefer to be?

5

An Egyptian pyramid builder

The pyramids were built to protect the tombs of the early pharaohs, the kings of ancient Egypt. There were once about 100 pyramids, most of them near Memphis, not far from modern Cairo. They were built in about 2650-2100 BC. A few were built later, further south up the river Nile, but none were built after 1640 BC. Instead, the later pharaohs were buried in the hillsides near their new capital which was at Thebes.

The first true pyramid was built in about 2650 BC. It is over 60 m high and is called the Step Pyramid, because it is shaped like six huge steps. We know the name of the builder, Imhotep, who designed it for the pharaoh Zoser. Imhotep was not only a builder; he was also the

The stone used to build the pyramids was cut by peasants or slaves, who worked full time at the quarries. First, men cut grooves into the solid stone using hammers and chisels. They then knocked wooden wedges into the grooves. When they poured water in, the wood became swollen and the stones split away from the rock face. The stones were cut to shape at the quarry and each one marked with the name of the gang that had cut it.

pharaoh's chief adviser and high priest. He was famed as a writer, an astronomer and a doctor, and after his death was made a god. Imhotep's pyramid, and the temples round it, were the first buildings ever made of large blocks of smooth stone. He showed the way for the building of later, even bigger, pyramids.

The Great Pyramid at Giza was built in about 2575BC for the pharaoh Cheops. It is made of 2.5 million stone blocks and is still the largest stone building in the world.

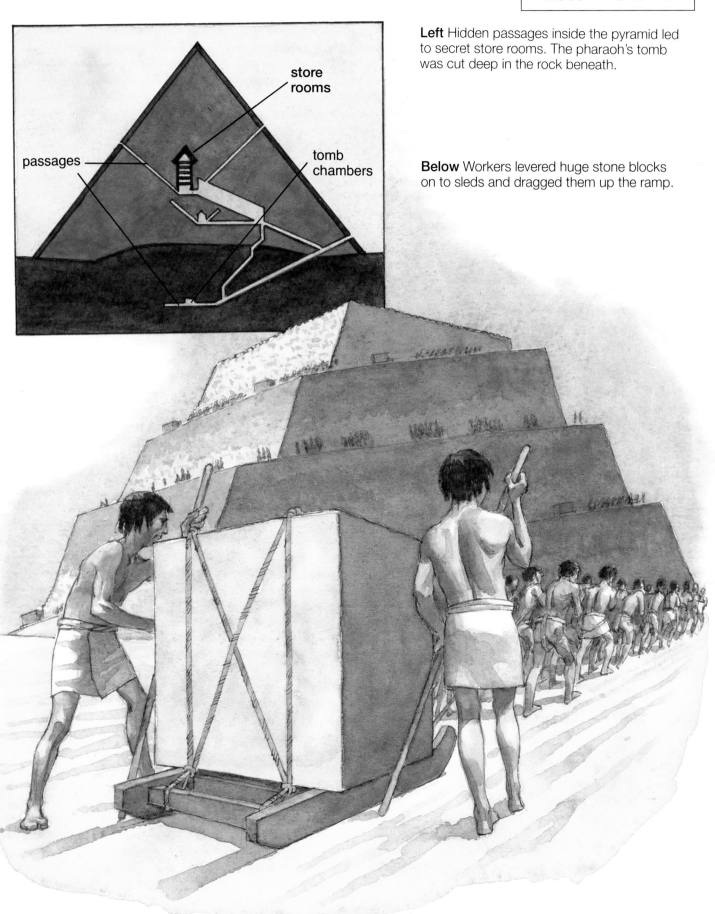

store
rooms

passages

tomb
chambers

Left Hidden passages inside the pyramid led to secret store rooms. The pharaoh's tomb was cut deep in the rock beneath.

Below Workers levered huge stone blocks on to sleds and dragged them up the ramp.

An Egyptian pyramid builder

Vast numbers of people were needed to build these amazing structures. The Greek writer Herodotus tells us that 100,000 men worked on the Great Pyramid at Giza. Some were peasants or slaves who worked full time at the limestone and granite quarries, digging out the stone. Most were poor farmers who were ordered to build the pyramid during the months when the Nile flooded the valley and farming was not possible. They worked in gangs of twenty-five men, supervised by soldiers. Each gang's job was to move the enormous ready-cut stones from the quarry to the building site, then raise them into position on the pyramid.

With the Nile in flood, the limestone blocks could be floated most of the way to the building site on barges. But the strongest stones, the huge blocks of granite used in the centre of the pyramid, came from Aswan, 966 km upriver. All year round, a fleet of boats sailed up to Aswan to collect the granite and drifted back to Giza on the river current.

At Giza, men cleared and levelled the building site and erected a smooth ramp from the water's edge to the pyramid. Workers levered the huge stone blocks on to sleds and dragged them up the ramp.

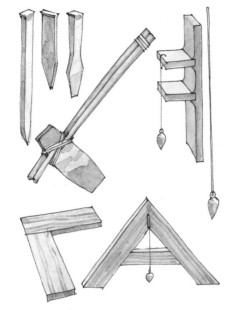

Above Some Egyptian builder's tools. Heavy tools like hammers, axes and big chisels were made from a hard rock called dolerite. Saws, drills and fine chisels were made of bronze. Builders only had simple plumblines, wooden set squares and rulers, but their measurements were accurate to within millimetres.

King Cheops and his pyramid
This account is by the Greek writer Herodotus (about 490-425 BC) who visited Egypt as a young man:
'Cheops brought the country all sorts of misery. He . . . compelled the people to labour as slaves for his own advantage. Some were forced to drag blocks of stone from the quarries in the Arabian hills to the Nile . . . The work went on in three-monthly shifts, a hundred thousand men in a shift. It took ten years of this oppressive slave-labour to build the track along which the blocks were hauled . . . To build the pyramid itself took twenty years . . . An inscription is cut upon it in Egyptian characters recording the amount spent on radishes, onions and leeks for the labourers.' (Herodotus, Histories, Book Two, transl. Aubrey de Selincourt, Penguin, 1954)

Below This Egyptian tomb-painting shows builders dragging stone blocks on wooden sleds.

Right Model houses made of clay were often buried in Egyptian tombs. This model of a craftsman's house shows the sort of home that the pyramid builders lived in. Egyptian houses were built of mud, which was shaped into bricks and dried in the sun. Pyramid workers lived in special villages of little houses like this. Mud bricks are easily damaged, so very few traces of these villages remain to be seen today.

Tomb paintings show workers pouring water under the sleds to make them slide more easily, or rolling them on logs.

Once the pyramid started to grow, the task became even more difficult. We still do not know for certain how the workers lifted the stones into place. Herodotus said they used wooden levers. But most people today think they used mud and rubble to build gently sloping ramps round the sides. The builders could drag the stones up these ramps on rollers. Unfortunately, there are no tomb paintings showing this part of the operation. The men used a thin layer of sticky mortar to slide each stone into place. At first, the pyramid's sides were stepped. But once the top stone was in position, the ramps were taken away, one level at a time. Triangular stones were then used to fill in the steps and give the pyramid its final smooth shape. The builders rubbed down the surface with small sandstone blocks for a really fine finish. At last the Great Pyramid was complete and ready for Pharaoh Cheops' body when he died.

Inside the pharaoh's tomb
H. V. Morton describes a visit to the Great Pyramid in 1937:
'It was one of the most sinister apartments I have ever entered, a really horrible place, and I could well believe that it might be haunted. The air was stale and hot, and the foul reek of bats so strong that I kept glancing up, expecting to see them hanging on the corners of the walls. Although this room is 140 feet [43 m] above the level of the sunlit sandhills outside, it gives the impression of being in the depths of the earth . . . It is indeed the darkness of the grave, and joined to the darkness was the silence of death.'
(*The Story of Architecture* by Patrick Nuttgens, Phaidon, 1983)

Left This is a mask of the boy-king, Tutankhamun. He was buried in the Valley of the Kings near Thebes in 1352 BC. When Howard Carter found the tomb in 1922, it still contained the pharaoh's mummified body. The mask was discovered inside the coffin. Food, furniture and jewellery had also been buried with him for use in the afterlife.

9

A Greek temple builder

In 480 BC, Persian invaders destroyed all the old temples on the Acropolis, the hill which stands above Athens. Temples were very important to the Greeks. They were not just places of worship, like churches today, but were homes for their gods and goddesses. The people of Athens wanted their goddess, Athene, the goddess of war, to have the most splendid temple of all. In 447 BC, Pericles, the leader of Athens, decided to rebuild the temples. The biggest is still called the Parthenon, which means virgin. It was named after the goddess, Athene.

You could say that the Parthenon had many builders. First there was Pericles himself, the ruler of Athens, whose idea it was. Pericles collected the money to build the temple from other Greek cities that Athens had helped in the wars against Persia. He made the sculptor Phidias responsible for the project.

Help from the Goddess
This story is told by the Greek writer Plutarch (about AD 45-120) in his *Life of Pericles*:
'*While the temples were being built . . . one of the workmen slipped and fell from a great height. He lay for some time severely injured, and the doctors could hold out no hope that he would ever recover. Pericles was greatly distressed at this. But the goddess appeared to him in a dream and ordered a course of treatment, which he applied, with the result that the man was easily and quickly healed.*'
(Plutarch, *Pericles*, from *The Rise and Fall of Athens* transl. I. Scott-Kilvert, Penguin, 1960)

It may seem odd to have a sculptor in charge instead of an architect. But the new temples were covered with incredibly beautiful sculptures, so it was important that the person in charge knew how to show them off well.

Left The Parthenon still stands out against the sky above Athens. Once there were many other temples and statues on the hill. The ruins on the left are the Propylaea, a huge gateway through which visitors approached the Parthenon. Today, smoke and fumes from the modern city are eroding the fine stonework of the ruins.

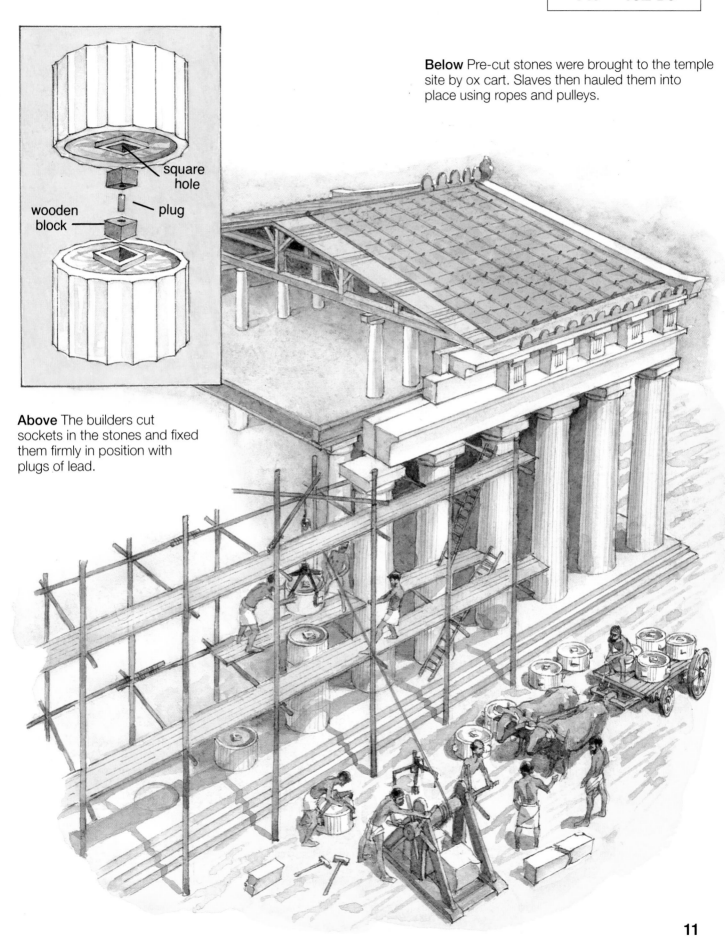

square hole

plug

wooden block

Below Pre-cut stones were brought to the temple site by ox cart. Slaves then hauled them into place using ropes and pulleys.

Above The builders cut sockets in the stones and fixed them firmly in position with plugs of lead.

A Greek temple builder

Next there were the architects, Ictinus and Callicrates, who designed the temple. They drew all the detailed plans and ordered the glowing white marble to be cut by the slaves who worked in the stone quarries outside Athens. These slaves were mostly foreigners from Europe and Asia. The Athenians may have bought them as children from their parents, or taken them prisoner during wars. The slaves had to work hard for their keep, but were not normally ill-treated. Many of the quarry slaves were highly skilled building workers. Their job was to cut all the stones roughly to shape. Then gangs of other slaves dragged along the cut stones on sleds. In

Below Marble pictures ran round the top of the inner wall of the Parthenon. They show people and horses taking part in a procession held in honour of Athene's birthday. This frieze, and the other sculptures on the temple, were probably designed by Phidias. Sculptors were paid six drachmas to carve each figure. When finished, the figures were painted in bright colours on a red background. In the nineteenth century they were bought by Lord Elgin and shipped to the British Museum, in London, where they can still be seen.

Fixing the stones
Greek builders did not use mortar. Instead they cut sockets into each marble block and joined them with iron clamps set in molten lead. Where the stones touched, the surfaces were so finely ground down with sand that only a hair-line was visible.

this way the stones were transported to Athens.

Lastly, there were the craftsmen who constructed the temple. Some of them were citizens – higher class Athenians who owned land and were allowed to vote in the Assembly.

The Parthenon today. In 1687, an explosion destroyed the roof and part of one side.

But most of them were called metics – free traders and craftsmen who could work for wages but not own land or vote. Citizens and metics usually owned a few slaves who did the less skilled jobs for them. Women were not allowed to do this sort of work. If you could travel back in time to visit the site you would probably see small groups of men – made up of citizens and metics, and their slaves – each working on one piece of stone. They were paid separately for each finished piece of stone by the magistrates who looked after the city's money. Some accounts for the work still survive, cut in stone, so we know the names of workers and how much each was paid.

Many people say that the Parthenon is the most perfect building ever constructed. It is under 70 m long, so is quite small. You could stand twenty-four Parthenons on the base of the Great Pyramid! But it was built with incredible accuracy, and has many surprises when looked at closely.

Phidias knew that our eyes do not always see things exactly as they are. They often distort our view of buildings, especially those that are high up, a long way off, or seen in strong sunlight. So, to make the Parthenon *look* perfectly straight and symmetrical, Phidias deliberately distorted its shape. The building seems to be rectangular, but there are no true right angles to be found in it. The horizontal lines, like the steps at the base or the pediment at the top, are not quite straight. Instead, they all curve upwards slightly. The columns are not straight either, but bulge outwards slightly in the middle. From far off this makes them appear straight. They also tip inwards, so that if you continued them upwards they would not meet until they were at least 1.5 km above the earth. In fact, though the Parthenon looks perfectly regular, no two blocks of stone are exactly alike.

Builders at Home
Most people in ancient Greece lived in simple houses made of mud bricks. From outside they looked plain, with almost no windows opening on to the street. But inside the rooms were colourfully painted, and faced on to a courtyard. The shaded colonnade round the yard was like a scaled-down version of the temple's tall columns. Girls and women spent most of their time here. They were not allowed to share the busy outdoor life of male citizens.

A Roman road builder

By AD 200, the Roman Empire stretched from Scotland to the Sahara Desert, and from Syria to Spain. It seems incredible that, without modern communications, the Romans were able to conquer and control such a vast area. It was in part thanks to their network of smooth, straight, well-maintained roads that they were able to do so.

The Appian Way, built in 312 BC, was the first major Roman road. It stretches 200 km south from Rome and was built for a blind government official called Appius Claudius. This road was so well made that it was still in good condition 900 years later.

Most of the 80,000 km of Roman main roads which we know about were built later, during the first two centuries AD. At this time the empire was still expanding. Good roads were essential. They enabled the government in Rome to keep in touch with what was happening throughout their territory. As soon as the army gained control over a new area, such as Celtic Britain in 43 AD, the soldiers began to build roads. Perhaps they did not feel secure until they could march safely and quickly from one fort or town straight to another.

The Romans probably did not have accurate maps. The only one that survives is a later copy of a sketch of the empire, made around AD 200, called the *Tabula Peutingeriana*. It shows roads in red. Unfortunately it does not show the true size, shape or position of the features marked. The *Itinerary of Antoninus,* also written around AD 200, is a list of main routes with distances in miles but without a map.

Many modern roads follow Roman routes, so they are very straight. Just look at this one in the Drôme, France.

A Roman road builder knew that stones must be shaped to fit tightly together and then hammered into place. Notice how the road is built up in layers of different materials.

The poet Statius (AD 45-96) welcomed a new road in southern Italy:
'In the past, our traveller, late, riding in his two-wheeled cab, was tossed back and forth . . . afraid of seasickness even in the middle of the country. No carriage could move swiftly as the muddy ruts hindered and slowed their passage . . . But now, a journey that used up a solid day barely takes two hours. Birds on their outstretched wings fly no more swiftly . . .'
(Statius, *Silvae* IV, iii. Quoted in 'These were the Romans', G.I.F. Tingay & J. Badcock, Hulton, 1972)

large blocks of hard rock

sandy concrete

gravel in clay

flat, squared stones in cement

Smoother, straighter roads also encouraged traders to bring luxury goods from across the empire, such as shiny red pots from Gaul or large quantities of fragrant olive-oil from Italy.

The most skilled road building work was done by soldiers. Surveyors and engineers travelled with every Roman legion. It was their job to choose the route and decide on construction methods. All soldiers were trained as builders, though the heavy digging work was sometimes done by gangs of local people or slaves. With as many as a thousand people working together, roads were built quickly, thanks to careful planning and strict discipline.

Roman roads are famous for being very straight. Later, road builders often had to build winding roads, to avoid cutting across fields or property. But the Romans did not need permission to build, and could choose the most direct route. In fact, Roman roads are rarely straight for more than a few kilometres at a time. Instead, they were built in a series of straight lengths from one hilltop to another.

A Roman glass perfume bottle. Goods like this travelled across the empire by road.

The surveyors built beacons, or fires, at high points, then set up marker poles in straight lines between them. Although each section of a Roman road is straight, quite noticeable angles can occur between sections. Often roads curved round hillsides or along river valleys, or even zig-zagged up hills. However, where possible, roads followed high ground, as this gave better visibility and avoided flooding. Many modern roads still follow Roman routes.

Once the surveyors had marked out a route, parallel ditches were ploughed. These ditches were up to 27 m apart, and the land between them was cleared of trees. Then the edges of the road were marked with two more ditches, usually about 9 m apart. Earth and rubble from the ditches were piled up in the centre to raise the bed of the road, making a low mound called an agger.

The Romans knew that a road's strength comes from its foundations rather than its surface. They therefore built on top of a heavy base of shaped stones fixed tightly together, sometimes with cement. Layers of smaller stones, flints and gravel followed.

A Pompeii Street
The seaside town of Pompeii in southern Italy was covered by volcanic ash in AD 79, and rediscovered in the 1700s. Typical Pompeian pavements were raised high to protect people from the dirt of the road. The blocks of stone prevented big carts from using the town streets.

Left: A typical Pompeian street.

Where possible, Roman roads crossed rivers at shallow fords. But bridges were needed to cross deep rivers. The Pont du Gard was built about 20 BC in southern France. The lower level still carries a main road; the upper levels were aqueducts to carry fresh water from mountain streams to the city of Nimes.

They were placed on top and rammed down firmly. These layers of stone were not placed evenly over the whole surface of the road, but were 'cambered' to give a gentle slope down each side. This ensured that water drained off into the ditches. It was important to avoid puddles, which might cause the road to break up in freezing weather.

Of course, all roads need regular maintenance. Even the best surfaces were eventually worn away or cracked by the iron-rimmed wheels of heavy carts. A government department in Rome called

Road builders

'What great gangs of men are working side by side! Some cut down the woods, and clear the mountain sides. Others are chiselling smooth the timbers and stones. Others are binding the rocks together with lava dust and cement and surfacing the work, or bailing dry the pools and diverting the smaller streams.'
(Statius, *Silvae*, IV, iii, ibid.)

the *curatores viarum* (carers of the ways) was responsible for repairs. The Roman roads that still survive usually show evidence of regular patching and resurfacing.

A Celtic house builder

Until about AD 100, tribes of Celtic people lived across most of Europe, from Scotland and Ireland down to Switzerland and Spain. Their builders used many different materials, choosing whatever was most easily available. In Scotland and Wales, for example, stone was plentiful. They used it to construct little stone houses called brochs, each with two storeys linked by a stone stairway. Animals were kept on the ground floor and families lived upstairs. You can still find small houses in Spain built to a similar plan.

But in most parts of the Celtic world, houses were made of wood – usually strong hardwood such as oak, and the roofs were thatched. These houses are usually called roundhouses, because they were often round in shape. On the continent of Europe, Celtic houses were sometimes rectangular, although roundhouses were stronger. They could stand more buffeting by wind and rain, though rectangular houses were more convenient to live in.

Whatever the shape of the house, the builders began by digging holes in the ground. They sank sturdy hardwood posts into these holes, to form the main weight-bearing frame of the house. A taller pole was erected in the middle to hold up the roof. Then the builders cut down willow or hazel trees. These woods are flexible and easy to split. They could be woven to make a sort of fence, which filled in the gaps between the main posts. The whole house was then daubed with a mixture of soil, clay, straw and animal dung. Once dry it became solid and made the house waterproof.

Left: A stone Celtic-type house at El Cebrero, Spain.

How to make daub
This recipe for daub was used to build a house at Butser. Add 40 bales of straw, the hair of 40 pigs, sundry brambles, grass, hay, roots and other vegetable matter, to 3.5 tonnes of clay and 3.5 tonnes of earth. In areas where there is no clay, use cow dung and chalk. Mix the ingredients with water and apply liberally by hand to the walls.

Roundhouse walls were woven like giant baskets then plastered with clay daub. This set hard and made the house weatherproof.

A Celtic house builder

A steeply sloping roof was built from thin tree branches, covered with straw or reeds, or even turf cut from the ground. The roof was at least 8m high, with a hole at the top for smoke to escape. It must have been very smoky inside when the fire was lit. There was usually only one doorway, perhaps with a small porch, but no windows. This was to keep the house warm. Most houses took about two weeks to build, from start to finish. Sometimes they were built by the families who were to live in them, helped by skilled carpenters and thatchers. Often, though, the whole house was constructed by craftsmen, usually helped by slaves.

Celtic houses were grouped together round the chieftain's hall. The chieftain's house was always the biggest. It

Inside a reconstructed Celtic house. Notice the loom (centre), grindstone (left) and central hearth (right).

might even have a second storey with a sun-room (an open balcony facing south), where the women worked during the day. Celtic villages were normally built on the tops of hills, surrounded by a ring of walls and ditches for defence against attack.

Lake villages
Some Celts lived in lake villages on boggy islands in the middle of lakes, as at La Tene in Switzerland. They made the bog stronger and dryer with layers of logs, brushwood, stones and clay. Round the edge of the village they built a high fence of stakes filled in with wattle and daub. It was very hard to attack a village that was built in this way. The lake dwellers used canoes to paddle to and from dry land and catch fish.

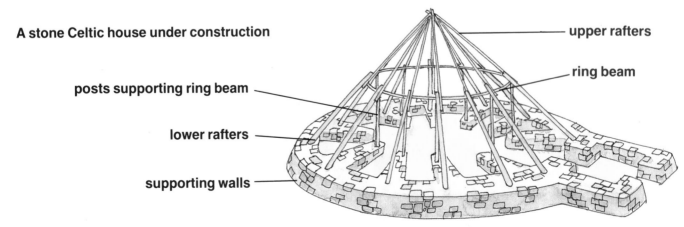

A stone Celtic house under construction

- upper rafters
- ring beam
- posts supporting ring beam
- lower rafters
- supporting walls

Celtic people were split into rigid classes. Builders were free craftsmen, on the same level as blacksmiths and farmers. Below them were poor labourers, slaves and captives from enemy tribes. Above them all came the Druids, warriors, nobles and the king. Druids were priests with great power over Celtic people. It was their job to make sacrifices to the Celtic gods to ensure, for example, good harvests or victory in war. In Anglesey, off the coast of Wales, they are even thought to have made human sacrifices.

This golden neckband, called a torque, was found buried in Norfolk, England. It was probably worn as jewellery by a chief of the Iceni tribe.

Hillfort settlements like this were amongst the earliest true villages or towns north of the Alps.

The ancient Celts did not use writing to communicate or record their ideas. It is only from archaeology that we know where and how they lived. Archaeologists believe that Celtic culture began in central Europe at Hallstatt in Austria and La Tene in Switzerland. Evidence from Hallstatt (700 to 500 BC), shows how the Celts began by using bronze to make their weapons and tools, but later discovered iron – a far more durable metal. However, they continued to use bronze for artwork and decoration. By 500 BC, when Celts were living at

La Tene, iron had almost completely taken over from bronze. For this reason the majority of historians refer to the Celts as Iron Age people.

Some historians have tried to discover more about the Celts by rebuilding their homes and living exactly as the Celts did 2,000 years ago. At the Butser Project in Hampshire, England, people built a whole village of Celtic houses to live in. Here they grew the crops the Celts grew, kept the same animals, used the same tools and ate the same foods. They were particularly surprised to discover that the Celts needed over 200 trees to build each house.

A Roman view of the Celts
The Romans were appalled by the way the Celts lived. The Romans lived in brick houses with glass in the windows and centrally heated floors. To them the Celts were no more than barbarians. This was how the Roman writer Tacitus described them: '*It is a well-known fact that the peoples of Germany never live in cities, and will not even have their houses set close together . . . Every man leaves an open space round his house, perhaps as a precaution against the risk of fire, perhaps because they are such inexpert builders. They do not even make use of little stone blocks or tiles. What serves their every purpose is ugly timber, both unimpressive and unattractive. They smear over some parts of their houses with an earth that is so pure and brilliant that it looks like painting or coloured mosaics.*'
(Tacitus, *On Britain and Germany*, transl. H. Mattingly, Penguin, 1948)

A medieval master mason

During the Middle Ages (about AD 1000 to 1500), the Roman Catholic Church was very rich and powerful throughout Europe. Many people willingly gave money to build magnificent cathedrals, abbeys and other churches for the worship of God. Their designers and builders were skilled craftsmen called master masons.

Master masons were usually responsible for buying stone and other building materials, and for organizing the workers on the building site. Sometimes they could even be found cutting stone themselves. But their main job was to draw the plans for the building. These included designs and moulds for all the complicated details and decorations, such as the fancy stone tracery of the windows. Pictures of master masons usually

Ely Cathedral, England, was planned by Abbot Simeon in 1083. These towers were finished in 1190.

show them holding drawing instruments – set squares, dividers and compasses. Unskilled building workers were called rough masons, whilst semi-skilled stone cutters were usually known as free masons.

Tools
Set squares were needed to draw and check angles; dividers were used to mark circles and measure lengths. A wooden template was cut for each section and held against a slab of stone while it was cut to shape. Simple numbers or marks were made on cut stones to show where they should go. In addition, each mason might make his own special mark. This would identify who had cut each stone.

These cathedral builders are using a huge treadwheel to hoist the stones into position. The wooden frame can be removed once all the stones of the arch are in place.

Master masons were highly paid, and the church authorities looked after them well. Often they were given houses, food and clothing while they were employed, and generous pensions to support them when they became too old or ill to work. Some masons owned stone quarries and charged the Church for the materials they supplied. To learn his trade, a mason became an apprentice, or pupil, of an experienced master. After about seven years he qualified as a journeyman. He then spent several years travelling from site to site improving his skills. Finally he might become a master mason himself, in charge of designing and building a new church or cathedral.

First the mason drew designs in ink on long rolls of parchment, prepared from thin sheep- or goatskin. He showed these to the Church authorities or whoever was paying for the building. The plans showed the dimensions of the different parts of the building. Often they followed a regular pattern which all masons understood. Next the mason marked out the plan on the ground.

Church builders about 1409. Notice the wooden scaffolding and pulley. The master mason's lodge is the thatched building at the back.

Cutting the stones

The heaviness of stone made it very difficult and expensive to transport, and carriage was often much more costly than the stone itself. To save money, most stones were cut to shape at the quarry. The master mason visited the quarry regularly to take templates (patterns) and check the work in progress. Each stone was given a special mark with a chisel to show the rough masons back at the site what it was for. Then the stones were carefully loaded into horse-drawn carts or boats for transport to the site.

This French stained-glass window was made in about 1485. It shows drapers preparing cloth for sale.

He hammered poles in at the corners, and stretched ropes between them to show where the walls would go. Internal details were marked on the ground with lime.

Many materials were required for the different parts of a church – stone and mortar for the walls, wood for beams, lead for the window frames and roof, glass for windows, perhaps tiles and bricks for the floor, as well as nails, ropes and baskets for the workers to use. Some of these materials were made or found locally. But others, like the high quality ashlar stone blocks needed for smooth wall surfaces, or dark marble stone for decorations, had to be brought from far away. Norwich Cathedral, in the east of England, was built partly from stone imported from France.

Deep foundations were needed to support the huge weight of the walls. Medieval masons did not take chances and many of their buildings have stood for almost a thousand years without serious problems. Building work usually started at the east end – the most important part of the building – which contained the main altars. Usually, work stopped for the winter on All Saints' Day (1 November) and the walls were given a thatched cover to prevent damage from rain and frost. Once the roof was on, work would continue under cover. A big cathedral could take a very long time to complete. Exeter Cathedral took seventy years to build, whilst Cologne Cathedral was left unfinished for five hundred years. During this time, many different master masons were in

Builders' tools from Spain, 1563. The picture on the previous page shows the tongs in use.

charge of the work, although they usually kept to the original plans.

Most medieval cathedrals were much bigger than any other buildings built before or after this period. Their tall towers and spires often still dominate the landscape. Inside, the great beauty of their pillars and sweeping arches has rarely been surpassed. They remind us of the astonishing skill of the masons who built them.

An Aztec builder in Tenochtitlan

There are no accurate accounts of the city of Tenochtitlan written by the Aztecs themselves. However, Hernan Cortez, the Spanish soldier who conquered the Aztecs, described the city in a letter to King Charles V of Spain:

'This city is so great and so beautiful that I can hardly say half of what I could say about it. It is even more beautiful than Granada.'

This was certainly high praise, as Granada was by far the grandest city in Spain at that time.

The Aztecs began to build Tenochtitlan in AD 1325, after two hundred years wandering through Mexico. They named the city after the prickly pear cactus fruit, which they had often eaten in the desert. For the site they chose a swampy island in the middle of Lake Texcoco, which they connected to the surrounding countryside by means of banks and bridges. Canals criss-crossed through the city centre, and were always busy with barge and canoe traffic. At the heart of the city they constructed an imposing central plaza. Many pyramids, crowned

An accurate reconstruction of an Aztec temple. Sadly all the real temples have long since been destroyed.

with temples, were built on this plaza. Most of these public buildings were made of white stone. This stone was purchased by the Aztecs from other tribes, as the Aztecs themselves had no stone.

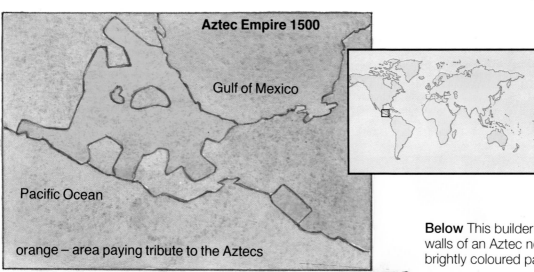

Aztec Empire 1500

Gulf of Mexico

Pacific Ocean

orange – area paying tribute to the Aztecs

Below This builder is decorating the walls of an Aztec noble's house with brightly coloured paintings.

The temples were painted with bright colours and decorated with gold, so that they sparkled in the sun. When the Spanish first saw the city from a mountain pass, it presented a breathtaking sight.

The Templo Mayor (main temple) dominated the central plaza. This was the most important building in the Aztec Empire, and was constantly altered over two hundred years. The main structure was a pyramid 30 m high, with two imposing temples perched on top. This is where their victims, usually prisoners captured in battle, were sacrificed to the gods.

Opposite the Templo Mayor on the main plaza was the king's palace. The king lived on the upper floor above the council offices, law courts and stores. All the walls were decorated with carvings and paintings, and the gardens and courtyards

In 1500, a terrible flood destroyed much of old Tenochtitlan. King Ahuitzotl rebuilt the city, making it stronger and more splendid than ever. Whole villages of workers were ordered to help the nobles rebuild their palaces, each one in a different style.

Tenochtitlan

'The city is spread out in circles of jaderadiating flashes of light like quetzal plumes.Beside it the lords are borne in boats: Over them extends a flowery mist.'(Nahuatl poem, quoted in *'Cortez and the Downfall of the Aztec Empire'*, John Manchip White, Hamish Hamilton, 1971, p. 99.)

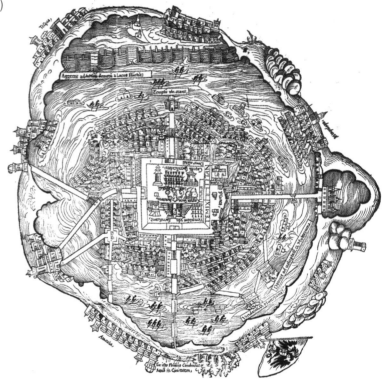

were dotted with cages of exotic birds and animals. King Ahuitzotl (1486–1502) took a special interest in building and was responsible for providing the money needed to complete work on the Templo Mayor. The heaviest jobs were done by slaves and *macehualli*, free labourers who had to work a few days each month for the government. The final decorations were added by well-paid craftsmen called *toltecs*.

Above This view of the city is based on a map drawn for Cortez, the Spanish conqueror. The main plaza at the centre contained palaces and about forty temples. Three raised roadways led across the lake to the city, but most transport was by water. The canals were laid out so that every part of the city could be reached by boat. There were several smaller towns round the shores of the lake. Including these, the total population may have been almost half a million people.

Tenochtitlan's many small islands were divided into areas lived in by different classes of people. A noble family's home was

The Aztecs built pyramids very similar to this one, constructed by the Teotihuacanos.

like an ancient Greek house (see chapter two), with a central courtyard used by the family when it was not too hot. On each side there were three or four rooms, each just one storey high. The richest nobles lived in palaces built of stone, covered with stucco (thin plaster) which was painted. But the usual building material was adobe – mud bricks dried in the sun, which were similar to those used in Mexico today. Slaves painted these buildings with whitewash to protect them and keep them cool. The famous Spanish soldier Bernal Diaz said they looked like 'gleaming white towers and castles – a marvellous sight.'

Poorer people lived on the outskirts of the city. The land here was so soft and swampy that it would not take the weight of stone or even mud bricks. Instead they built light-weight homes using wattle and daub, like the Celtic homes. They gathered rushes from the lake, wove them together and plastered them with a

The Aztecs believed that the world would end if the gods were not given a constant supply of human blood. Most victims were slaves or enemy soldiers captured in battle. They were taken to the top of the pyramid, and made to dance in front of the temple. Then the Aztec priests cut out their victims' hearts with a black stone knife. They rolled the bodies down the steps of the pyramid to the bottom, where butchers cut them up for food. In 1494, 20,000 men, women and children were sacrificed here in just four days, until the whole city stank of blood. Not surprisingly, the other tribes of Central America were glad when the Spanish eventually defeated the Aztecs.

covering of mud. Often, many family members, including uncles and aunts, grandparents and children, lived together in groups of small houses.

A Georgian house builder

In the 1700s, a new style became popular. Today we call these buildings Georgian, after the four King Georges who ruled England at that time. They are also called classical, as their design is based on the temples of classical Greece (see chapter two). There are classical-style buildings in almost every old city in Europe and North America, including the Kremlin in Moscow, Buckingham Palace in London and the White House in Washington. But the classical style was not just for grand public buildings like these. The front of Thomas Jefferson's house in Virginia, USA, was built in 1770 to look like a Roman temple. Soon, ordinary people wanted their houses built in this fashionable style too.

Georgian houses had a balanced look. The front door was normally placed

Above Monticello, President Thomas Jefferson's house in Virginia, USA, is shown on this five cent coin. Jefferson was an amateur architect who designed his own house in 1770. Its classical style was based on the ancient Roman buildings Jefferson saw during a visit to Italy.

in the centre, with an equal number of windows on either side. Sometimes the front door was framed by pillars, rather like the slender pillars on the front of a Greek temple. Over the door, supported by the pillars, was a triangular pediment – again, just like a temple. The windows were usually squares, or rectangles placed on end,

Advice to builders
Some architects published books or ideas and plans for local builders to copy. In *The Complete Body and Architecture* (1756), Isaac Ware warned against using red bricks in front walls: *'the colour itself is fiery and disagreeable to the eye; it is troublesome to look upon it; and in summer, it has the appearance of heat that is very disagreeable.'* Most builders ignored this advice.

Eleanor Coade's secret
From 1722, a new building material became available – Coade Stone. This was a type of cement, moulded to look like stone, made to a secret formula by Mrs Eleanor Coade. Her catalogue listed 778 different items, such as doorway pillars and statues. Unfortunately, the secret formula was lost when the business closed in 1837.

divided into square panes of glass. They normally opened by sliding up or down on sash cords rather than opening outwards on hinges. Most importantly, Georgian houses had to look solid, so they were built of brick or stone.

Speculative building – a safe bet?
Most houses were not built to order. Instead, builders speculated (risked their money) by putting up rows of houses, hoping to sell them at a profit when finished. To tempt buyers, builders sometimes built an impressive façade, or house front, on a plot of land. The rest of the house was built later, often badly and from inferior building materials. Some small Georgian houses were so poorly built that dancing in upstairs rooms was forbidden. The builders were afraid that too much vibration would make the houses collapse.

A Georgian carpenter using a special tool to tighten the cords of a sash window. Many of his tools are like modern ones, but we no longer use wooden scaffolding poles.

A Georgian house builder

Most pre-Georgian houses were not built like this. In many places, stone was unavailable and bricks were far too expensive. Until the 1700s, most houses were built with a timber frame filled in with wattle and daub. But the supply of hard oak wood was now beginning to run out, and bricks were becoming cheaper. Local builders learned how to lay bricks and began to build in the new style.

Of course, people did not suddenly knock down all the old timber-framed houses and build new, fashionable homes. Instead, they altered the older buildings to make them look Georgian, at least from the front. There were two ways they could do this. Old window frames could be replaced by new sash windows. The original front entrance was usually towards one end of the house. This could be blocked up and a new Georgian door built in the centre.

The biggest problem was the timber frame itself. The cheapest way to hide this was to cover it with a very smooth plaster.

The Renaissance

From the late 1400s, many European artists, architects and writers rediscovered the ideas of the Romans and ancient Greeks. We call this period the Renaissance, which means re-birth. Italian architects such as Andrea Palladio (1508-1580) designed great houses and churches in the Roman style. These were in turn copied in northern Europe and America. In the 1700s, rich gentlemen liked to travel to Italy on a grand tour. When they returned home they sometimes rebuilt their homes in 'palladian' style.

Compare the Georgian house below with the ruins of ancient Rome on the right. Can you see the similarity?

Above This is a picture of the Royal Crescent (1767) in Bath, England. From a distance, it looks like a vast palace. Close up, you can see that it is a terrace of thirty separate homes. They were designed by John Wood to give middle-class people the illusion of living in a grand country house.

This plaster looked like stone. But people with enough money usually preferred a different solution. They used bricks to build a whole new wall in front of the old one. From the street it was hard to tell that it was not a new house.

While some Georgian builders were busy with alterations to old houses, many more were building new ones. In the century after 1730, the population of Britain rose from seven million to seventeen million people. Some other European countries grew almost as fast. Never before had there been such a demand for new houses.

Almost every village now had its own brickworks supplying hand-moulded bricks and tiles to local builders. The builders usually worked in small firms of just three or four men, with a variety of skills between them. As well as bricklayers and tilers, they needed skilled carpenters to make and fit windows, panelled doors and planked floors. House buyers now expected smooth walls and decorative cornices round ceilings, so builders needed to be expert plasterers too. Sometimes they had to do plumbing work with lead (the word plumber comes from *plumbus*, the Latin for lead) on pipes, gutters and roofs. Some big towns now had piped water supplies and sewers, and these needed expert fitting to avoid leaks.

Most importantly, builders had to learn to design houses in the fashionable Georgian style. Why not try to find out about the famous architects of the eighteenth century – people like William Kent in England and Charles Bulfinch in America? These people were not interested in designing small houses for ordinary people. This was part of the job of the builders themselves. The popularity today of Georgian-style houses is a tribute to the skill of their builders.

A nineteenth-century builder in iron

The world's first iron bridge was built across the River Severn in Shropshire, England, by Abraham Darby in 1781. People could see that iron gave exciting opportunities to build on a bigger scale than ever before. Iron parts were light in weight but very strong for their size. They were made in factories, then taken by rail and quickly assembled on site. Builders learned how to be engineers, and the modern age of building began.

Prince Albert, Queen Victoria's husband, wanted to have an industrial exhibition in London in 1851. But there was no building large enough to hold it. So a competition was announced to design an exhibition hall to be built in Hyde Park, central London. There were three main problems to solve. The building must be the biggest in the world. It was

Above Abraham Darby's bridge at Ironbridge Gorge (completed in 1781) was the first large structure ever built of iron.

to be taken down again once the exhibition was over. And it had to be built very quickly, as time was running out. 245 designs were entered, but all were too solid or too ugly. Then an unusual plan appeared in a magazine. Its designer was a gardener called Joseph Paxton. His idea resembled a huge green-house and the judges soon declared it the winner.

Washington Roebling supervising work on the Brooklyn Bridge in 1876. The men on the platform are using a winding machine to cover the main suspension cable with thinner wires.

The building of the Brooklyn Suspension Bridge

Paxton had proved that an iron building could enclose a vast area. In 1867, an American called John A. Roebling and his son Washington Roebling showed how iron could be used to span a great distance – the mouth of the Hudson River between New York and Brooklyn. The Roeblings' Brooklyn Suspension Bridge had a single span of 500 m. At each end, 90 m-high towers were built and four thick cables strung between them. The road and railways were then hung from these, 40 m above the river.

Over 200 men worked on the project. First they dug deep underground to sink the base of each tower down to solid rock. Then they worked high overhead, joining together thousands of heavy wires. Over twenty men died due to accidents during this dangerous work. But by 1883 the bridge was finished.

A nineteenth-century builder in iron

Just seven months later the Crystal Palace, as it was nicknamed, was finished. The iron frame weighed 4,500 tonnes. It was made in small sections 193 km away and taken to London by train. Once the frame was up, 293,655 panes of glass were carefully lifted into place. A 33 m-high dome was built in the centre to cover a large old elm tree growing on the site.

Thanks to Paxton's idea, the Great Exhibition opened on time on 1 May 1851. Three years later, the Crystal Palace was taken down again and rebuilt in south London. Sadly, it was destroyed by fire in 1936.

Sir Joseph Paxton
Paxton was born in 1803. On leaving school he became a gardener's boy. He proved so good at his job that in 1826 he was made Head Gardener by the Duke of Devonshire. In 1846 he designed a special iron and glass house to house a giant water-lily, and this became the model for the Crystal Palace. He sketched the Palace on blotting paper during a meeting, and drew all the plans in nine days. Paxton also wrote books, started a newspaper, directed a railway company, and in 1854 became a member of Parliament. He died in 1865.

Iron was used for the world's biggest and longest buldings around the mid- to late 1800s. Soon the tallest building would be of iron too. The French government wanted a really spectacular building for the Paris Exhibition of 1889. They asked a bridge builder called Gustav Eiffel to design a 300 m-high tower.

The Eiffel Tower has a graceful, simple shape. But it is really a giant jigsaw with 18,038 pieces! Each part had to be separately drawn and made in workshops 5 km from the site. Eiffel deliberately designed the iron parts to be small. None weighed over three tonnes, and all measurements were accurate to a tenth of a millimetre. 250 workers used steam-powered cranes to help raise the pieces into place. As the tower grew taller, special cranes were fixed to the ribs of the tower itself.

Opinions about the Crystal Palace
Queen Victoria was impressed by the Crystal Palace. She wrote in her diary, 'The building is so light and graceful in spite of its immense size . . . the effect is quite wonderful.' She described the opening as 'one of the great days in all our lives'. Not everyone agreed. In April 1852, Colonel Sibthorp told the British Parliament, 'The very sight almost sickens me . . . stuffed with foreign fancy rubbish. The Crystal Palace is a transparent humbug. The sooner the thing is swept away the better.'
(*Palace of the People*, Graham Reeves, Bromley Library Service, 1986.)

The Crystal Palace was built around a large elm tree growing on the site.

Iron bridge disasters

Some early iron buildings became unsafe in strong winds. In America, 251 railway bridges broke up in ten years. In Scotland, the Tay Bridge collapsed in 1878 while a train was crossing during a storm. The train was lost and all seventy-five passengers drowned in the river below.

Wooden platforms gave the men a safe foothold while they joined the parts together with bolts and rivets. The people of Paris were amazed at how quickly the tower grew, and it was complete in only two years. Unlike most buildings, the Eiffel Tower was finished on time, cost less than expected, and caused the loss of only one life – a young man who slipped while showing off to his girlfriend. Today, visitors can still take the lifts to the first and second platforms. But you would need to be very fit and have a good head for heights to climb the 1,671 steps to the top!

Gustav Eiffel

The Eiffel Tower (right), was designed by Gustav Eiffel for the Paris Exhibition in 1889. However, this was not his first success. He also designed New York's most famous landmark, the Statue of Liberty. The figure is hollow, held up by an iron skeleton. It was shipped to New York in eighty-five huge cases and set up there in 1885.

An American sky-scraper builder

From the 1880s, business was booming all over the western world. Nowhere was this more obvious than in the great American cities of Chicago and New York. Land in the city centres was scarce. Its cost was so high that there seemed to be only one place for new shops and offices to go, and that was upwards. By 1893 a new word had entered our language – skyscraper.

In 1871, a terrible fire reduced most of the centre of Chicago to a heap of smoking ruins. As the city was gradually rebuilt over the next thirty years, architects and builders discovered new ways of constructing ever taller blocks of offices, homes and shops.

However, very tall buildings presented serious structural problems. All their weight – their walls, floors, roofs and contents – was

Above New York's famous skyline is dominated by its skyscrapers, many built during the 1920s. Zoning laws insisted that they should taper towards the top to avoid casting huge shadows over the buildings all around them.

Fast construction
Skyscrapers were built very quickly from ready-made parts, which could be quickly bolted or riveted together. In just ten days, the Empire State Building rose fourteen floors. With the framework in place, builders could add floors and walls at many different levels at the same time.

normally carried by the outside walls. The higher a building went, the thicker these walls needed to be, especially at the base, Very tall buildings therefore needed huge amounts of brick or stone, and the areas of their lower floors were limited. One solution to this problem had already been tried on a small scale in Britain. Since the 1790s, some factories and mills had been built with floors resting on iron beams supported by strong iron columns.

A skyscraper needs a strong foundation. This can be a solid concrete raft if the ground is very firm (a). Otherwise, different types of steel piles can be driven deep into the earth to get a good grip (b and c), or rest on solid rock (d).

a)

b)

c)

d)

A builder bolts the ready-made framework of a towering skyscraper together.

Fire
The Chicago fire of 1871 showed how easily metal parts can twist, causing buildings to collapse. To prevent this, a skyscraper's frame was usually covered in hollow tiles or concrete to protect it from heat.

An American skyscraper builder

In 1883, the American engineer William Jenney used a similar method to construct the Home Insurance Building in Chicago. He claimed that this system could be used for buildings of almost any height. Though Jenney's building was only ten storeys high, he had built the world's first proper skyscraper.

Jenney's solution was a simple one. The floors of the Home Insurance Building were held up by a skeleton of vertical and horizontal iron girders. These were bolted together with angled brackets, rather like the Crystal Palace. From outside, the

Skyscrapers were born in Chicago, but in New York they soon reached much greater heights. In 1926, the seventy-two storey Chrysler Building was the first to exceed the Eiffel Tower as the world's tallest building. The most famous skyscraper of all, the Empire State Building, was built in 1929-31, with 103 storeys and a height of 378 m. Only recently has this record been broken, by the 443 m-high Sears Tower, back in the skyscraper's birthplace of Chicago.

The Chrysler Building, New York. Can you see how this skyscraper is a huge advertisement for the motor company?

The pyramids (chapter one), the medieval cathedrals (chapter five) and the Eiffel Tower (chapter eight) were undoubtedly very tall buildings. But they were all pointed in shape. Their upper sections were never intended to provide usable space. Nobody wanted to live or work in buildings more than a few storeys high because of all the steps they would have to climb. But the invention of powered lifts (1852-1900) and telephones (1876) made it possible to move people and information quickly up and down buildings of almost any size.

control gear
lifting motor

main cable

guide rails

safety brake

counterweight

floor buffer

Lifts
In 1856, Elisha G. Otis installed the first passenger lift in a New York store. It was raised and lowered by a rope wound round a steam-powered drum. If the rope snapped, an automatic brake stopped the car falling. The invention of the electric lift in 1880 made it possible to construct even taller buildings.

walls of the Home Insurance Building look like any traditional building. In fact, they are quite thin and light, resting on ledges sticking out from the iron framework hidden inside. William Jenney proved that the skyscraper's iron construction could be built quickly, efficiently and cheaply. The thin, lightweight outside walls also allowed very big windows, helping to make office blocks more light and airy.

Other builders soon developed Jenney's ideas further. William Holabird and Martin Roche's thirteen-storey Tacoma Building had an all-steel framework. This was both stronger and lighter than Jenney's mainly iron construction. Steel beams could be held together by rivets, which were quicker to fix than bolts. Most importantly, the Tacoma's foundations were made from steel piles set in concrete. This was another vital development, as the higher buildings are, the stronger their foundations need to be.

Until the 1890s, most skyscrapers still looked like huge versions of traditional buildings.

Lloyds Building, London, 1986
A century after the first skyscrapers were built, office buildings are still pointing upwards. Richard Rogers designed this one 'inside out'. The working parts, such as lifts and heating plants, are fixed on the outside. They use less space there, and will be easier to replace.

The new methods of construction were hidden behind thin but solid-looking stone walls. Louis Sullivan, another Chicago architect, saw that the taller buildings became, the more heavy and ugly they looked. Sullivan wanted his skyscrapers to look good, so he hung thin, pale-coloured tiles on the outside surfaces. These could make any pattern, and need not look like blocks of stone.

A modern energy-efficient house builder

People have always built their homes with energy in mind. The Celtic chieftain's house in chapter four, for example, had a thatched roof. Thatch is a good insulator, so it kept the house warm in winter but cool in summer. During the day, the chief's family sat in the southern side of the house, to make the most of the natural warmth of the sun. Centuries later, the New York authorities insisted that skyscrapers were built so that they did not cast shadows which would make surrounding buildings permanently cold and dark. It has always paid to make the most of the free energy the sun provides.

The generation of energy using coal, oil and gas is costly, and producing it damages the environment. Yet a third of all the energy we make goes to heat our homes, and much

In sunny countries, people often put solar panels on their roofs to make hot water for their homes.

of that is wasted. An older house, like a Georgian house, uses four times as much energy as a modern house. Even today, most houses could be much more energy-efficient.

When the sun shines through big windows, it can quickly warm up a room. Some builders now plan their houses to make use of this heat. The kitchen faces east to catch the morning sun. By the afternoon, the sun has moved towards the west. This makes a good position for a living room where people can sit in the evening. The cold north side of the house is kept for rooms which are not lived in, or which need less heat, like entrance halls or spare bedrooms.

cold water in

Sun's rays

glass

insulation

black absorber plate

pipes

hot water out

Below A modern builder fits a solar panel to the roof of a new house. Solar water heaters, like the one on the left, can also be mounted on the roof.

A modern energy-efficient house builder

The benefits of the sun's heat can be greatly increased by building a glass conservatory on the sunny side of the house. During the summer this provides useful extra living space. When it becomes too hot, an automatic heat recovery system pipes the surplus heat to other parts of the house. The same system is designed to recycle hot air extracted from kitchens and bathrooms.

The rear wall of the conservatory can be made of a dense material like concrete which absorbs and stores heat. At night the wall cools, giving off heat into the house and providing free warmth twenty-four hours a day.

Even in winter, the conservatory traps some warmth and helps to insulate the house.

Not all the energy we use in our homes goes on heating rooms. Some is used to heat water or power electrical appliances such as lights and cookers. Builders today can use the sun to help do these jobs too.

Solar water heaters use sunshine to produce hot water. Some people make their own out of old radiators. They paint the old radiators matt black to absorb heat and mount them in a sheltered, sunny place. Factory-made solar heaters are now efficient enough to supply much of a family's hot water needs

through most of the year. Solar panels, usually fixed on house roofs, can also be made to turn light into electricity. This can be stored in batteries for use when the sun is not shining.

Insulating materials work by trapping still air in bubbles, or between the strands of a substance like fibreglass wool. The air

Waste
Modern life produces mountains of waste. Much of this could be re-cycled to save energy. Straw can be made into boards for building or lining walls. In Sheffield, UK, household waste is burned to produce steam which heats thousands of nearby homes. In Sweden and Denmark, many people have special toilets which convert human waste into gas or garden compost.

Know your U-value
Builders can calculate the heat lost from different parts of a house using a scale called the U-value. The higher the number, the more rapidly the heat is lost. Here are examples:

Single-glazed window **5.6**
double-glazed window **2.8**
solid brick wall **2.0**
cavity brick wall **1.5**
roof with 25 mm fibreglass **0.9**
roof with 150 mm fibreglass **0.2**

Right This diagram shows a heat recovery system. Warmth otherwise lost from the kitchen and bathroom is used to pre-heat the fresh air supply to the living room.

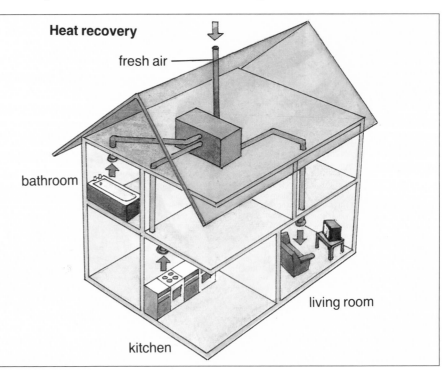

Heat recovery

fresh air

bathroom

living room

kitchen

Most of the energy we use in our homes is wasted. Heating a house is like running a bath with the plug out. Almost as fast as we heat up the house the heat runs out again. Eventually, all the heat we put in ends up outside. Modern builders are concerned to slow down this wasteful heat loss. Draught-proofing windows and doors is a cheap way to prevent warm air escaping. It can save about ten per cent of heating costs. But in most houses built before the 1980s, far more heat is lost through walls, windows, floors and roofs. Proper insulation of these areas can dramatically reduce fuel bills. This builder is filling the wall cavity with a special insulation substance.

trapped in a double-glazed window cuts heat loss by half. Extra layers of glass reduce heat loss still further. An uninsulated roof loses ten times as much heat as one with 150 mm thickness of insulating material. Much of the heat lost through walls and floors can also be saved – the thicker the insulating material, the more heat it keeps in. The Rocky Mountain Institute is in Colorado, USA, where the temperature can fall as low as −40°C in winter. Yet the building is so well insulated that it needs almost no heating apart from the body heat of its occupants. Enough electricity was saved in just ten months to cover all of the extra insulation costs involved.

Glossary

Angled brackets   Triangular metal plates used to join iron girders together.
Archaeology   The study of ancient remains.
Architect   Someone who designs buildings.
Assembly   An official meeting for making laws.
Astronomer   Someone who studies the stars and planets.
Conservatory   A sun room built mainly of glass.
Dividers   An instrument with two points to measure short lengths.
Energy-efficient   Making the best use of energy.
Engineers   People who design or build machines or large structures.
Fibreglass wool   Fluffy padding used to reduce heat loss from buildings.
Formula   A recipe for making something.
Gradients   Measures of the slope up or down a hill.
Inscription   Words cut or marked on a building or a coin.

Insulator   A substance which protects, or reduces heat-loss.
Mortar   Cement for holding bricks or stones together.
Palladian   The building style begun by the Italian architect Palladio.
Parchment   Sheep- or goatskin specially prepared for writing on.
Pediment   Triangular-shaped piece below the roof end of a building such as a temple.
Piles   Poles driven deep into the ground to support a building.
Plumblines   Lead-weighted strings used to check that walls are vertical.
Rivets   Iron rods driven through two metal pieces, in order to join them together.
Solar   To do with the sun.
Solar panels   Devices for turning the sun's rays into heat or electricity.
Surveyors   People who measure or test land or buildings.
Tracery   A type of fine stone decoration which is found in church windows.
Zoning laws   Rules which say how far apart tall buildings must be.

Further reading

GENERAL BOOKS

Brown, D, *The Kingfisher Book of How they were Built* (Kingfisher, 1991)
Courtenay-Thompson (Ed.), *The Visual Dictionary of Buildings* (Dorling Kindersley Books, 1992)
Gaff, J (Ed.), *Tell me about Buildings, Bridges and Tunnels* (Kingfisher Books, 1991)
Whitlock, R, *Exploring Buildings* (Wayland, 1987)
Yarwood, D, *A Chronology of Western Architecture* (Batsford, 1987)

BOOKS ON PARTICULAR PERIODS

Vanags, P, *Empires and Barbarians* (Usborne, 1990)
Macauley, D, *Pyramid* (Collins, 1988)
Macauley, D, *Cathedral* (Collins, 1988)
Coldstream, N, *Medieval Craftsmen – Masons and Sculptors* (British Museum Press, 1991)
Dineen, J, *Young Researcher – The Aztecs* (Heinemann, 1992)
Vale, B and R, *Green Architecture – Design for a sustainable future* (Thames and Hudson, 1991)

Timeline

Some of the major developments in the history of builders and buildings.

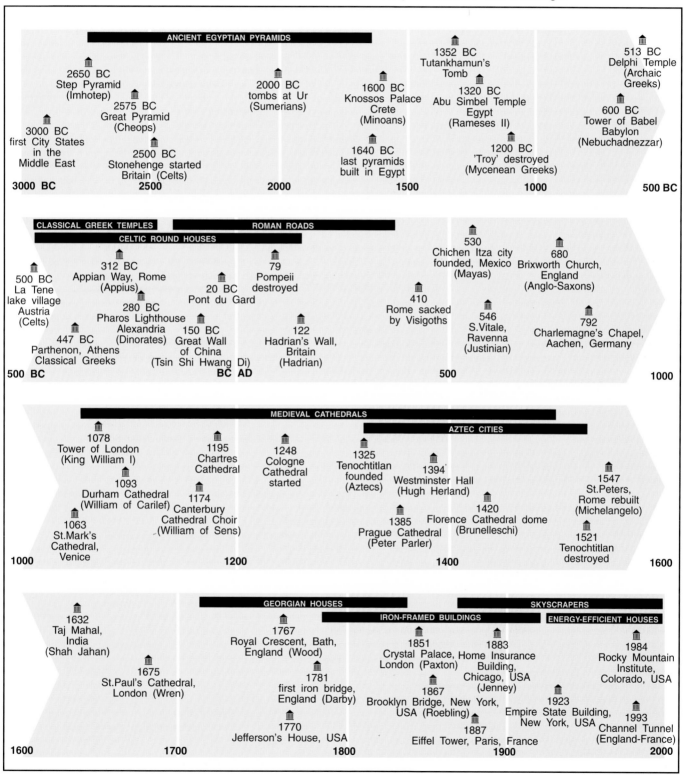

ANCIENT EGYPTIAN PYRAMIDS

2650 BC
Step Pyramid
(Imhotep)

2575 BC
Great Pyramid
(Cheops)

3000 BC
first City States
in the
Middle East

2500 BC
Stonehenge started
Britain (Celts)

2000 BC
tombs at Ur
(Sumerians)

1600 BC
Knossos Palace
Crete
(Minoans)

1640 BC
last pyramids
built in Egypt

1352 BC
Tutankhamun's
Tomb

1320 BC
Abu Simbel Temple
Egypt
(Rameses II)

1200 BC
'Troy' destroyed
(Mycenean Greeks)

513 BC
Delphi Temple
(Archaic
Greeks)

600 BC
Tower of Babel
Babylon
(Nebuchadnezzar)

3000 BC · 2500 · 2000 · 1500 · 1000 · 500 BC

CLASSICAL GREEK TEMPLES · **ROMAN ROADS**
CELTIC ROUND HOUSES

500 BC
La Tene
lake village
Austria
(Celts)

312 BC
Appian Way, Rome
(Appius)

280 BC
Pharos Lighthouse
Alexandria
(Dinorates)

447 BC
Parthenon, Athens
Classical Greeks

20 BC
Pont du Gard

150 BC
Great Wall
of China
(Tsin Shi Hwang Di)

79
Pompeii
destroyed

122
Hadrian's Wall,
Britain
(Hadrian)

410
Rome sacked
by Visigoths

530
Chichen Itza city
founded, Mexico
(Mayas)

546
S.Vitale,
Ravenna
(Justinian)

680
Brixworth Church,
England
(Anglo-Saxons)

792
Charlemagne's Chapel,
Aachen, Germany

500 BC · BC AD · 500 · 1000

MEDIEVAL CATHEDRALS
AZTEC CITIES

1078
Tower of London
(King William I)

1093
Durham Cathedral
(William of Carilef)

1063
St.Mark's
Cathedral,
Venice

1195
Chartres
Cathedral

1174
Canterbury
Cathedral Choir
(William of Sens)

1248
Cologne
Cathedral
started

1325
Tenochtitlan
founded
(Aztecs)

1385
Prague Cathedral
(Peter Parler)

1394
Westminster Hall
(Hugh Herland)

1420
Florence Cathedral dome
(Brunelleschi)

1547
St.Peters,
Rome rebuilt
(Michelangelo)

1521
Tenochtitlan
destroyed

1000 · 1200 · 1400 · 1600

GEORGIAN HOUSES · **SKYSCRAPERS**
IRON-FRAMED BUILDINGS · **ENERGY-EFFICIENT HOUSES**

1632
Taj Mahal,
India
(Shah Jahan)

1675
St.Paul's Cathedral,
London (Wren)

1767
Royal Crescent, Bath,
England (Wood)

1781
first iron bridge,
England (Darby)

1770
Jefferson's House, USA

1851
Crystal Palace,
London (Paxton)

1867
Brooklyn Bridge, New York,
USA (Roebling)

1887
Eiffel Tower, Paris, France

1883
Home Insurance
Building,
Chicago, USA
(Jenney)

1923
Empire State Building,
New York, USA

1984
Rocky Mountain
Institute,
Colorado, USA

1993
Channel Tunnel
(England-France)

1600 · 1700 · 1800 · 1900 · 2000

Index

Celebrating Weddings
Around the World

Anita Ganeri

raintree

a Capstone company — publishers for children

Raintree is an imprint of Capstone Global Library Limited, a company incorporated in England and Wales having its registered office at 7 Pilgrim Street, London EC4V 6LB – Registered company number: 6695582

www.raintree.co.uk
myorders@raintree.co.uk

Text © Capstone Global Library Limited 2016
The moral rights of the proprietor have been asserted.

Edited by Clare Lewis and Brenda Haugen
Designed by Richard Parker
Picture research by Gina Kammer
Production by Helen McCreath
Originated by Capstone Global Library Ltd
Printed and bound in China by CTPS

ISBN 978 1 406 29896 3
19 18 17 16 15
10 9 8 7 6 5 4 3 2 1

British Library Cataloguing in Publication Data
A full catalogue record for this book is available from the British Library.

Acknowledgements
We would like to thank the following for permission to reproduce photographs:
Alamy: © Danita Delimont, 9, © ephotocorp, 11, © SFM Italy, 13; Capstone Press (map), throughout; Capstone Studio: Karon Dubke, 28, 29; Corbis: Godong/© Robert Mulder, 21; Getty Images: Avinash Achar, 16, Burke/Triolo Productions, 20, Holger Leue, 8, Jodi Cobb, 27, Kevin Winter, 5, Maremagnum, 7; Glow Images: Exotica, 10, PhotoNonStop/Sébastien Boisse, 25, Superstock, 14; Newscom: Jochen Tack imageBROKER, 15, Juan_Herrero European Press Agency, 26, Peter Langer/Design Pics, 17, REUTERS/LEE JAE-WON, 18, REUTERS/MOHAMED AL-SAYAGHI, 19, Robert Harding/Tuul, 6, Robert Harding/Tuul, 12, ZUMAPRESS/Du Boisberranger Jean, 24; Shutterstock: S-F, 23, Sergey Ryzhov, 22, silentwings, cover

We would like to thank Dr Suzanne Owen for her invaluable help in the preparation of this book.

Every effort has been made to contact copyright holders of material reproduced in this book. Any omissions will be rectified in subsequent printings if notice is given to the publisher.

All the internet addresses (URLs) given in this book were valid at the time of going to press. However, due to the dynamic nature of the internet, some addresses may have changed, or sites may have changed or ceased to exist since publication. While the author and publisher regret any inconvenience this may cause readers, no responsibility for any such changes can be accepted by either the author or the publisher.

Contents

Some words are shown in bold, **like this**. You can find out what they mean by looking in the glossary.

Getting married

In cultures around the world, important events in people's lives are marked with special customs and ceremonies. They help people to celebrate occasions, such as the birth of a baby, a wedding or to remember a person who has died. They are also a way of guiding people from one stage of their lives to the next. This book looks at how people from different cultures and religions celebrate weddings.

All over the world, weddings are happy occasions which the bride and groom often want to share with their friends and family. There are usually special clothes to wear and special foods to eat, including many different types of wedding cakes. In some cultures, people exchange rings or other jewellery. There are also many customs for finding a partner.

OVER THE BROOM

In some African-American families, couples end their wedding ceremony by jumping over a broomstick. This tradition dates back to the days of **slavery** when slaves were not allowed to get married officially. "Jumping the broom" showed that they wanted to be together.

This African-American groom and his new wife are "jumping the broom".

Beauty contest

The Woodabe tribe live in Niger, West Africa. They are cattle herders who move from place to place to find food and water for their animals. Once a year, they gather together at the edge of the Sahara Desert for a very unusual beauty contest.

Young Woodabe men wear colourful clothes and make-up for their dance.

Young Woodabe women watch the men dancing and choose one as a husband.

The young men paint their faces and put on colourful costumes, made from beads and shells. Then they stand in lines, link arms and dance for hours in the hot desert sun. The men roll their eyes to make them look bigger and grin to show off their teeth. They wear black lipstick to make their teeth look whiter. Some men also wear headdresses, decorated with ostrich feathers to make them look taller.

The aim of the contest is to find a woman to marry. The women watch the men dancing and pick who they think is the most handsome as their husbands.

COLOUR CODING

The colours of the dancers' make-up have special meanings. Red is the colour of blood. Yellow is the colour of magic. Black is the opposite of white – the colour of death. The black paint is made from the bones of a bird called the **cattle egret**.

Leap of faith

On the islands of Vanuatu in the South Pacific Ocean, men have a daring way of showing off to possible girlfriends. They jump off a wooden tower, some 30 metres (98 feet) high. They have only two **vines** tied around their ankles to stop them crashing to the ground. The aim is to swing as low as possible, just grazing their shoulders on the ground. The jumpers hope that the more daring they are, the more impressed the women will be.

North America

Europe

Asia

Africa

Equator

South America

Vanuatu

Australia and Oceania

Antarctica

A jumper leaps from the wooden tower, held up by only two vines.

The tower takes about four weeks to make, with the whole village helping. The ground underneath is dug over to make it softer for landing. Platforms are built at different heights, the lowest at around 10 metres (33 feet) above the ground. On the night before the jump, the men sleep underneath the tower to scare away evil spirits.

On the day of the jump, the men wash and rub themselves with coconut oil. They wear boar tusks around their necks. They cross their arms over their chests and tuck their heads in, to avoid injury. Then they jump, reaching speeds of more than 70 kilometres (43 miles) per hour as they dive.

Villagers gather around the tower, singing and dancing, to show their support for the jumpers.

Sacred steps

Many **Hindus** marry someone chosen for them by their families, although the boy and girl must agree with their parents' choice. A priest looks at the couple's **horoscopes** and decides on a lucky day for the wedding.

On the wedding day, there are around 15 different **rituals** to be performed. The ceremony is led by a priest who reads from the **sacred** texts and lights the sacred fire. The bride and groom follow the priest's instructions but they do not speak to each other.

The Hindu bride and groom walk around the sacred fire.

During the ceremony, the priest ties the groom's scarf to the bride's **sari** to show that they are joined for life. The bride places her foot on a special stone to show that she will stand firm for her husband and family.

The most important part of the ceremony comes near the end. The couple take seven steps around the sacred fire. With each step, they make a vow for food, good health, wealth, good fortune, children, happiness and life-long friendship. The couple are now married.

WEDDING NECKLACE

To show that she is married, a Hindu bride wears a black and gold necklace. It is called a mangala sutra, which means "lucky thread". She also paints a red mark on her forehead.

This mangala sutra is ready for the wedding ceremony.

Sikh
wedding

Sikh weddings often take place in the **gurdwara**. The bride and groom bow to the Guru Granth Sahib, the Sikh holy book, before sitting down. The bridegroom wears a long scarf, called a pulla, around his neck. After readings and prayers, the groom takes one end of the pulla and the bride the other. This shows that they are now joined together.

During the ceremony, the bride holds one end of the groom's pulla.

During the wedding ceremony, the Lavan (wedding hymn) is read. The four verses are spoken, then sung. As each verse is sung, the bride and groom walk around the Guru Granth Sahib. When they have done this for a fourth time, they are married. The guests shower them with rose petals to congratulate them.

The bride and groom walk around the Guru Granth Sahib.

WEDDING HYMN

This is the first verse of the Lavan:

"In this first circle, God has shown
  you the duties of family life.
Accept the Guru's word as your guide
And it will make you free from sin.
Meditate on the name of God,
Which is the theme of all the scriptures.
Devote yourself to God and all evil
  will go away.
Blessed are those who hold God in
  their hearts.
They are always happy and content."

Shinto wedding

Shinto is an ancient religion that many people still follow in Japan. Its followers believe in spirits, called **kami**, that live in animals, plants and places such as rivers and mountains. They honour the kami at special **shrines**.

Shinto weddings take place at a shrine and are led by a Shinto priest and the miko (female shrine **attendants**). Only close friends and family are invited. At the beginning of the ceremony, everyone stands and bows, and the priest says prayers for the couple.

The bride, groom, priest, miko and guests make up this Shinto wedding procession.

WEARING WHITE

A Shinto bride wears a white **kimono** and a large, white hood. Tradition says that the hood covers up her "horns of jealousy" so that she can start her new life with her husband.

This Shinto bride and her groom are wearing traditional dress.

Afterwards, the bride and groom drink an alcoholic drink, called sake. They take turns sipping from three different-sized cups – small, medium and large. The first two times, they only raise the cups to their lips. They take a drink on the third time. Then the couple stand near the **altar**, and the groom reads out the wedding **oath**.

The ceremony ends with the miko giving the couple a **sacred** branch, which they put on the altar as an offering to the kami. They also exchange rings.

Wedding Clothes Around the World

Wedding colours

In Western countries, many brides wear white on their wedding day. In Britain, white dresses became very popular after Queen Victoria's marriage to Prince Albert in 1840. The Queen wore a white lace dress. Before that, brides had worn many different colours, such as blue, yellow, black and brown.

In many Eastern cultures, red is a lucky colour. A **Hindu** bride usually wears a red silk **sari** because red is the colour of blood, and of life itself. Her hands and feet are decorated with delicate patterns, painted in a red dye called mehndi (henna).

A Hindu bride also wears beautiful wedding jewellery.

Wedding rings

Many people exchange gold rings during their weddings, as a sign of their love for each other. They wear the rings on the fourth fingers of their left hands. In ancient times, people thought that a vein led from this finger straight to the heart.

The bride and groom wear crowns during part of the ceremony.

Marriage crowns

In the Eastern Orthodox Church, the bride and groom have beautiful gold crowns placed on their heads. The crowns show that they are now linked to each other and to God. The crowns are taken off at the end of the ceremony.

Mass wedding

Getting married is one of the most special days in a person's life. Many couples enjoy being the centre of attention, with their friends and family helping them to celebrate. Other couples like to get married in large groups, with hundreds of other brides and grooms.

The Unification Church of South Korea holds huge wedding ceremonies for its members.

There are hundreds of brides and grooms at this mass wedding.

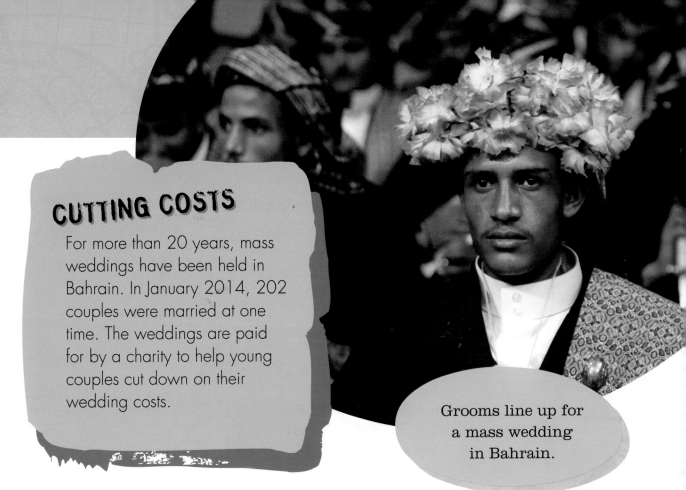

Grooms line up for a mass wedding in Bahrain.

In February 2000, some 60,000 people got married at a mass wedding held in the Olympic Stadium in Seoul, South Korea. They came from 150 different countries. For thousands of the couples, it was the very first time that the bride and groom had ever met each other.

At the ceremony, the couples were sprinkled with holy water. Then they said their wedding vows and exchanged rings. The ceremony ended with a firework display. Until his death in 2012, these mass weddings were led by the Church's leader, Reverend Sun Myung Moon. They are now led by his wife, Hak Ja Han.

Breaking glass

A traditional **Jewish** wedding begins with the bride and groom signing the ketubah (say "kett-oo-bah"), or marriage **contract**. This sets out the promises that the couple make to each other for a long and happy life together.

This Jewish bride and groom are standing under a huppah.

During the ceremony, the couple stand under a special canopy, called a huppah. The huppah is a sign of the new home which they will share. It is closed on top for privacy but open on all sides as a sign that others are welcome inside. The **rabbi** makes a speech about the couple, and says seven blessings, one for each of the seven days of creation. He also blesses a glass of wine and gives it to the couple to drink.

The ceremony ends with the groom stamping on a wine glass with his foot. This is said to be a reminder of the destruction of the Temple in Jerusalem, the Jews' holiest place, almost 2,000 years ago. It shows the couple that there will be sad times ahead as well as happiness.

MAZEL TOV!

Afterwards, the guests call out "Mazal Tov!", which means "Congratulations!" in **Hebrew**. The day ends with a party, with lots to eat and drink, and plenty of singing and dancing.

Everyone joins in the dancing at the wedding party!

Wedding Food

Around the World

Wedding cakes

At weddings in the United Kingdom and North America, there is usually a splendid wedding cake. The cake is a sponge or fruit cake, decorated with white icing and often topped with figures of the bride and groom. It is made in different layers. The top layer may be saved for the couple's first anniversary or the christening of their first child.

The bride and groom cut their wedding cake together.

Guests at weddings in Brazil are given "bem casados" ("happily married") cakes to take home. These are made from two pieces of sponge cake, joined together with caramel cream or jam. They show how the couple are joined together as husband and wife.

Chicken soup

In Germany, people eat a special wedding soup called Hochzeitssuppe. It is a clear chicken soup, with pieces of chicken, small meatballs, asparagus, noodles and boiled egg. It is eaten with slices of raisin bread.

Decorated bread

Korovai is a large, round, plaited loaf of bread, served at weddings in the Ukraine. It is often decorated with birds, which represent the couple and their family and friends. The loaf is surrounded by periwinkle leaves, a symbol of love.

This korovai has periwinkle leaves on it. They are a symbol of love.

Wedding festival

Every year in September, the Berber people of Morocco hold a special festival in the region of Imilchil, high up in the Atlas Mountains. Thousands of people come from the villages all around to look for husbands and wives. The festival lasts for three days and people camp out in the valley. There is a **bazaar** where people can buy clothes and other goods, and a market where sheep, goats and donkeys are sold.

These Berber girls are dressed up for the Imilchil festival.

The grooms sing and dance as they wait to meet their future wives.

At Imilchil, the girls dress up in their finest clothes and best silver jewellery. The boys wear white turbans and long robes. By the end of the festival around 40 couples are ready to get engaged. If a boy and girl like each other, their families meet in a tent to discuss the arrangements for the wedding, which is celebrated another day.

LAKES OF TEARS

There is a sad story behind the festival. Legend says that a boy and girl from different tribes fell in love. However, they were not allowed to marry because their families were enemies. The two cried themselves to death, filling two lakes with their tears. In their grief, their families set up the festival so that boys and girls from different tribes could meet.

Civil
weddings

A **civil wedding** is a wedding that has nothing to do with religion. It can take place in a **registry office**, or another place that has been registered for weddings, such as a castle or hotel. The couple invite their friends and family, and may choose readings, poems, music and songs, as part of the ceremony. A civil wedding means that a couple are married according to the law.

Civil ceremonies can even be held in an aquarium!

In some countries, the civil ceremony may be only one part of a wedding. It shows that the couple are legally married, but they may have a religious ceremony, too.

This couple are travelling by helicopter to their wedding in the Grand Canyon, USA.

Some people choose to have their weddings in places that are special to them, such as on a beach or in the countryside. Others choose unusual places to get married, such as in a zoo or aquarium, or deep under the sea, wearing scuba diving gear.

Fold a **Japanese** paper **butterfly**

YOU WILL NEED

• Rectangle of pretty paper, with a different colour or pattern on each side

At a Shinto wedding, the bride and groom sip sake from cups decorated with paper butterflies (see page 15). These are some of the oldest origami designs. Follow these steps to make your own paper butterflies.

1 Fold the paper rectangle in half lengthways. Crease and unfold.

2 Fold the paper in half again the other way.

3 Put your thumb inside the top right corner. Open up the paper and bring the corner across to touch the fold in the middle. Squash the paper flat, into a triangle shape.

4 Turn the paper over, and do the same on the other side.

5 Turn the shape upside down. Fold the inside corners down, crease, and unfold.

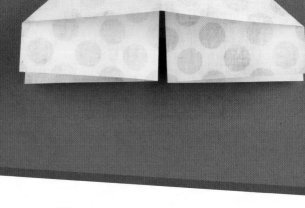

6 Fold down the front layer of paper on each side. Press down to flatten the wings.

Make butterflies in lots of different colours and patterns. Use them to decorate wedding cards and gifts.

Glossary

altar place where offerings such as food and flowers are made to gods and ancestors

attendant person who helps the priest in the Shinto religion

bazaar another word for market

cattle egret small bird that picks ticks and flies from cattle

civil wedding wedding that is not religious but legally binding

contract agreement between people

gurdwara Sikh place of worship

Hebrew language in which the Jewish holy books are written

Hindu person who follows the Hindu religion

horoscope chart showing the position of the stars and planets at the time of a baby's birth

Jewish connected with the religion of Judaism. A Jew is a person who follows Judaism.

kami spirits in the Shinto religion that are found in nature

kimono traditional Japanese silk dress

oath solemn promise

rabbi Jewish religious teacher

registry office place where civil weddings can take place, and where births, marriages and deaths are recorded

ritual ceremony with set ways of doing things

sacred special, usually to do with religion

sari traditional dress worn by many women in India

shrine holy place linked to a religious leader, god or saint

Sikh person who follows the Sikh religion

slavery when people are forced to work for others for no money and are owned by them. In the past, people from Africa were taken to the United States and forced to work as slaves.

vines plants with long, dangling stems

yam plant that has underground parts called tubers that can be eaten

Find out more

Books

Around the World in 500 Festivals, Steve Davey (Kuperard, 2013)

Encyclopedia of World Religions (Internet-linked Encyclopedias),
    Susan Meredith (Usborne, 2010)

What Do You Believe? Aled Jones (Dorling Kindersley, 2011)

Websites

www.bbc.co.uk/nature/humanplanetexplorer

This brilliant website has stunning photos and video clips showing how people live around the world. There is a section on life events, including birth, childhood, coming of age, finding a partner and death.

www.bbc.co.uk/religion/religions

Find out more about the world's religions on this fact-packed website. There is also an interfaith calendar which looks at celebrations and holy days in different cultures.

Further research

Have you ever been to a wedding? What was the ceremony like? Can you find out more about how people celebrate weddings around the world? What do the bride and groom wear? What do people eat? You can look in books, on the internet or ask your friends.

Index

Index